The I AM Journey Journal

Transformation
by Laurie Wondra

Standard Text:

Cover Design and cover photo by Laurie Wondra
Steps of Nature photo taken on a magical trail near the North Shore of Minnesota

If you would like to book Laurie as a guest speaker, classes, or for private appointments, contact her at www.YourLifeCore.com

Introduction

You are an energetic being. You have a frequency and you vibrate in frequencies that communicate throughout the universe. Frequencies have sound and color associated to them and this is how you communicate to everything around you. Your energy field communicates messages before you speak. Your energy enters the room before your physical being does.

Everything has frequency, so you are essentially always communicating with everything around you. Being aware of how energy works, and being able to facilitate energy helps you direct your life.

The earth's frequencies continue to elevate each year and therefore by your existence on earth your frequencies are elevating. You may feel these shifts with ease or through intense times of growth.

Some may term this process as the 'awakening 'process, but you are already 'awake'. This is a lifetime to remember your gifts and to exercise them. You are here to observe this awakened state and to use this knowledge to enjoy and heighten this experience.

I AM an energetic being in transformation
I AM a loving energy that loves unconditionally
I AM human with a spirited soul
I AM beautiful
I AM open to all that the universe provides
I AM an intelligent and learning being
I AM the voice of my truth
I AM a caring spirit
I AM true to my internal spirit
I AM authentic
I Am a teacher
I AM light
I AM balanced in my energy
I AM living a life of abundance
I AM at peace with the world
I AM without fear
I AM moving forward on my journey
I AM courageous
I AM a lifelong learner
I AM a giver and I AM a receiver
I AM balanced
I AM conscious of all elements of the earth
I AM connected to all the energetic realms
I AM loved
I AM the giver of love and light
I AM.. IAM

I AM Energy

From birth on we are constantly formulating concepts and ideas about ourselves based on our experiences with the people in the world around us. When we are very young, those people are most likely our parents and siblings because they are the ones with whom we spend the most time. By the time we are about five or six years old we have formulated our perception about ourselves based on the feedback we have gotten from others.

We have created a story about who we are and then continue to go through life looking for evidence to support that story. As we grow older our outer life becomes a direct reflection of how we feel about ourselves.

Your beliefs are areas you focus on consciously or subconsciously . They create the I AM energy and form who you are. They become the truths you speak and live. They are what you focus on, and how you form your life. You can shift your life by using the laws of energy to focus your thoughts, your beliefs, and create a new 'I AM'.

With this understanding, a refocus of your energy, and setting new intents you are able to align to that which you want to create. This is manifestation.

Focus and Process

What you focus on is where your energy is directed. You are a magnetic that holds power and intensity and when directed can shift your everyday experiences in life.

As an energetic magnet you draw to you like energies. If you vibrating at a high frequency energy you draw that like high frequency toward you. If you are a low frequency energy you draw that low frequency energy toward you. Your natural energies are normally high, so when vibrating at a low frequency it will take more energy to return to your normal state. 'Doing the work' is figuring out what pulls or drains your energy fields and what feeds or elevates your energy field and then correcting it.

As magnetic energies, you have the ability to manifest the life that you want, deserve and desire and you do so by the Universal Law of attraction. Your thoughts become words, become actions, become how you live as you draw like frequency to you.

When you set your intents, and you focus your energy, you are able to manifest and live the life that you desire.

Inspiration

May this journal inspire you to embark on a path of focus, setting intents, watching them manifest and in this process shift your life as it aligns to what you wish, desire and ask for.

The 7 Natural Laws of the Universe

The Law of Attraction is just part of the seven natural laws of the Universe. Of the Seven Laws, the Law of Vibration. may be the most important in how your everyday life plays out, what you attract and how you are able to manifest in your life.

Knowing what the seven laws are and how they work can make a significant difference in applying them to create the life you truly desire.

The Law of Vibration states that everything vibrates and nothing rests. Vibrations of the same frequency resonate with each other, so like attracts like energy. Everything is energy, including your thoughts. Consistently focusing on a particular thought or idea attracts its vibrational match.

How to apply it: Focus on what you want instead of what you don't want.

The Law of Relativity states that nothing is what it is until you relate it to something. Point of view is determined by what the observer is relating to. The nature, value, or quality of something can only be measured in relation to another object. You use internal reference material based on your personal past experiences to assist in measuring.

How to apply it: Practice relating your situation to something worse than yours, and you will feel good about where you are and bring perspective to the situation. Your worst may not be someone else's worst. This law relates to your personal point of view.

The Law of Cause and Effect states that for every action, there is an equal and opposite reaction. Every cause has an effect, and every effect has a cause. All energies remain in balance. Be at cause for what you desire, and you will get the effect. All thought is creative, so be aware of what you wish for and the effect it will bring.   Whatever you put out in the universe is what comes back to you. If what you want is happiness peace, joy, friendship, love.. then you should live 'being' happy, peaceful, joyful, loving and a loyal friend.

How to apply it: Consistently think and act on what you desire to be effective at getting it.

The Law of Polarity states that everything has an opposite. Hot-Cold, Light-Dark, Up-Down, Good-Bad. In the absence of that which you are not, that which you are… is not. Polar opposites make existence possible. Two halves equal whole. If what you are not didn't coexist with what you are, then what you are could not be. Therefore, do not condemn or criticize what you are not or what you don't want.

How to apply it: Look for the good in people and situations. What you focus on, you make bigger in your life.

The Law of Rhythm states that everything has a natural cycle. The tides go in and back out, night follows day, seasons, and life regenerates itself. We all have good times and bad times, but nothing stays the same. Change is constant and continual. Knowing that "This too shall pass" is great wisdom about life's ebb and flow.

How to apply it: When you are on a down swing, know that things will get better. Think of the good times that are coming.

The Law of Gestation states that everything takes time to manifest. All things have a beginning and grow into form as more energy is added to it. Thoughts are like seeds planted in our fertile minds that grow and bloom into a physical experience if we have fed and nourished them. Feeding and nourishment comes from belief and affirmation.

How to apply it: Stay focused and know that your goals will become reality when the time is right.

The Law of Transmutation states that energy moves in and out of physical form. Your thoughts are creative energy. The more you focus your thinking on what you desire, the more you harness your creative power to move that energy into results in your life. The Universe organizes itself according to your thoughts. It produces based on your thoughts.

How to apply it: Put your energy and effort, your thoughts and actions into attracting what you desire, and you will surely attract the physical manifestation of that energy. Note that if you focus on what you don't want, the universe will equally deliver as well.

Other Forces of Energy

The universe supports your purpose and your life goals. There are simple elemental energy laws of frequency that provide support and knowledge for you. When you understand these forces you can put in place practices and build tools that help you utilize these frequencies.

1. **Frequency of Creation**. Life doesn't just happen it requires your partnership. It requires your action and participation. You cannot wait for life to happen to you. The universe is interactive. You connect with energies of the universe and the universe expects action and movement. Patience is great, but BE and DO and the universe will respond.

2. **The Frequency of Growth.** Wherever you go there you are. For you to grow in spirit, it is you who must change and not the people places or things around you. The only given you have in your life is YOURSELF and that is the only factor you have control over. This is understanding of self. When you change who and what you are within your heart your life changes too.

3. **The Frequency of Responsibility**. Whenever you see, feel or believe there is something wrong, you are

experiencing something within yourself that you do not like. You mirror what surrounds you and what surrounds you mirrors you. You must take responsibility for what is in your life. If you don't like how you are or what you experience, start by shifting how you interact with this feeling and the understanding that this is a universe mirror, and therefore something within yourself you do not like.

4. **The Frequency of Humility**. What you refuse to accept will continue for you. Let go of trying to control . If what you see is an enemy or someone with a character trait that you find to be negative, this is judgment and does not allow you to see what is truly in front of you. This limits you on seeing a higher level of existence. All that is presented to you is an opportunity to learn and to accept that which is present.

5. **The Frequency of Connection.** Universe is connected. Everything we do is connected. Whether we believe it to be inconsequential and not important it is very important in the flow of energy in the universe. Everything has purpose and each step leads to the next step and so forth and so on. There is no one step more important as all steps are equal in energetic balanced.

6.   **The Frequency of Focus.** You can't think of two things at the same time. When your focus is on spiritual values it is impossible for you to have lower thoughts such as greed or anger.

7.   **The Frequency of Belief.** If you believe something to be true then sometime in your life you will be called upon to demonstrate that truth. The universe must deliver on our truths.

8.   **The Frequency of Past.**   Look back only to review what would have prevented you from being fully in the present moment. Past thoughts, patterns of behavior, and old dreams, prevent you from having new ones.

9.   **The Frequency of Change.** History repeats itself until you learn the lessons that you need to change your path. Examples and opportunities become more intense or more frequent if this lesson must be learned before you can move forward. You may feel frustrated or stuck if your soul knows it is time to move forward but you have not yet learned the lesson.

10. **The Frequency of Patience and Reward..** All rewards require initial work or action. Rewards of lasting value and impact require patience and at times persistent work. Be in a place of joy as you anticipate the coming of the reward.

11. **The Frequency of Inspiration.** You get back from something whatever you've put into it. The value of something is a direct result of the energy and intent that is put into it. Every persons contribution is also a contribution to the whole. Lack luster contributions have no impact on the whole or work to diminish it. Loving contributions lift up and inspire the whole

12. **The Frequency of Presence**. Be happy, be in gratitude and at peace in this present moment. If you are not, how will you ever be happy, in gratitude and at peace with any future moments for you are calling those moment to you NOW.

Three Easy Ways To Raise Your Vibrational Frequency

Raising your personal vibration rate not only helps you live life with greater ease, but it also affects the collective consciousness of earth in a positive way. There are simple ways to raise your frequency and begin the process of attracting like energy.

1. Connect with nature – Go for a walk outside in nature and connect with mother nature. In nature you can experience a closer connection with the natural frequency of mother earth. Mother earth is a natural healer, allowing you to release energy that doesn't fit your natural state. When you release old energy, mother earth infuses you with new energy. It is possible to feel a deep sense of peace and oneness when you connect with nature because your energies are restored to your natural state and you are in balance with that of the earth. As you learn to connect and appreciate nature, you allow your consciousness to rise up.

2. Get your body moving – Exercise and dancing will raise your consciousness by promoting healthy brainwave patterns, healthy neurotransmitter levels, and great circulation throughout your nervous system. Help yourself break the pattern of *not* exercising by going for a walk alone or with other, or even going dancing. Both examples are easy, fun, and empowering movement that release, infuse and elevate your inner frequency.

3. Simple meditation - Whether you are an advanced or a beginner, the benefits are tremendous and will allow you to tap into your highest state of conscious functioning. It is an act that will definitely raise your conscious awareness and allow you to attain greater focus, discipline, and develop a deeper joyous connection to life. Meditation can be short or long, with movement or non-movement, such as walking-meditation. The key is to carve out time to be present in your energy.

Six way of 'Being' that assist your transformation

1. Pursue higher intelligence - There are many ways to become more intelligent. Not everyone is intelligent in every area of their life. Some people are more emotionally intelligent, some have a higher I.Q., while some are more spiritually intelligent. All forms of intelligence increase and enhancements will help you on your journey towards expanding your awareness and becoming a more conscious human being.

2. Treat yourself with respect - Having respect for yourself and your actions will ultimately boost the amount of love that you express towards yourself and others. Make wise, respectful decisions that reflect your values and have strong respect for your personal beliefs. Treating others with respect will help you become a more conscious human being too, but before you can respect others properly, you must first learn to show the utmost respect towards yourself.

3. Practice forgiveness - Forgiving yourself can be very difficult sometimes: especially if you are operating in a lower state of consciousness. Realize that in order to rise up, advance, and become a more conscious person, you must be compassionate and forgiving towards yourself. Any hateful thoughts or pent up negative emotions that you may be holding towards yourself need to be released. Negative thoughts and emotions can easily lower your level of consciousness if you do not practice compassion and forgiveness.

4. Challenge your belief system - This one can be difficult for many individuals due to the influence of imprinted beliefs by their parents or guardians during childhood. Some examples of beliefs that you could change include: dietary (changing to a vegetarian), spiritual (from Christianity to Atheism – or vice versa), emotional (from sadness to happiness), etc. By changing your belief system and experimenting with new beliefs, you make yourself more conscious of life's endless possibilities.

5. Pursue a path of love - Pursuing a path of love and compassion and becoming more loving will aid you considerably in the process of becoming a more conscious human being. Never be afraid to add a new practice to your life – you never know what may be most effective or a life changing experience.

6. Express gratitude - Expressing gratitude on a daily basis is a very positive, fulfilling exercise to practice. Ways to express gratitude on a daily basis include: giving thanks for your food, expressing gratitude for yourself and others through prayer (as discussed earlier), complimenting others, and letting another person know that you are thankful for having them in your life. By sharing and expressing gratitude, you feel extremely satisfied and will become more consciously aware of the things that you truly appreciate in life.

Please Use the space below to create your I AM Statements.

These are the truth statements of how you see your I AM presence today.

I AM

I AM

I AM

I AM

I AM

I AM

I AM

I AM

I AM

I AM

I AM

I AM

I AM

I AM

Circle those which you intend to keep !

Please Use the space below to create your NEW I AM Statements.

These are the truth statements of where you desire to shift.

I AM

I AM

I AM

I AM

I AM

I AM

I AM

I AM

I AM

I AM

I AM

I AM

I AM

I AM

Please Use the space below to create your NEW *Directional-* I AM Statements.

These are a combination of current I AM that you will keep, and those from your NEW list that you will shift.

I AM

I AM

I AM

I AM

I AM

I AM

I AM

I AM

I AM

I AM

I AM

I AM

I AM

I AM

The Power of Focus :

Where you focus is where your energy is directed. For example, if you focus on how much you dislike your job or relationship, that is what you attract to you and where your energy flows. These are low frequency energies and as you draw any low frequency energies to you to, they begin to ooze into other areas or domains of your life.

Low energy frequencies are abnormal for your existence therefore they leave you feeling stuck, unclear and in most cases simply unhappy.

When you focus high frequency energy, or positive energy in your domains of life, you draw to you positive energy. In this heightened space of energy you are happy, joyful, at peace, and calm. High frequency energies are where you are meant to exist and they are where the planet vibrates to. When you are in these energies you are more in alignment with your authentic self and the frequencies of earth.

When you focus energy you establish the intent of where your energy will flow. This is known as setting your intents.

Where you focus - your energy follows

Make a **list** of words you might want to focus on, or use as an overall theme to where you direct your energy.

Now circle or highlight **one or a few words** that you might use as symbolic to what you want to bring in to focus. Make any adjustments to your I AM statements if needed.

Begin

*Where you **focus** - your energy flows*

Energy is a magnet to like energy

Use the Laws of the Universe to manifest

*what you want to focus on by setting your **intents**.*

The Universe Reacts

The universe provides, look for it,
know it happens if it's for your highest purpose

When it shows up and if it's not what you thought
you wanted
see what you were to learn, and adjust your intent

Don't give up

Intents

The state of a person's mind that directs his or her actions toward a specific object, goal, or state of being.

Intent is a derivative of INTEND - to have in mind as something to be done or brought about; planned, purposed, or designed

Our thoughts become our words become our actions, and it's how we experience life.

As human beings our external experiences tell us how we have grown, or transformed.

We interact with our external world in ways that serve our spiritual growth. We manifest our external world or these experiences. We have the ability to manifest or draw to ourselves that which we think we need . However we also have the ability to draw to ourselves that which we 'don't want' if the focus of our energy is there.

Be purposeful in setting you focus of intents.

What about unintentional intents ?

1. Someone sets an intent for you .....

They may unintentionally make a statement such as
you look so tired today....
you must feel really badly about this....

Making statements such as above have the impact of
pushing lower energy towards that person. These are
assertions and we may have unknowingly sent lower
energy.

2. Words don't match your inner thoughts or feeling.

This occurs when your words say one thing and your
thoughts say another thing. Your outer self is not aligned
with your inner self. They are in conflict.

Your words - I really want to do this
Your thoughts - how am I ever going to do this?

In this situation no matter what your *word*'s are, your
thoughts are what shifts your energy.

**Thoughts becomes words, become action become how
you live.**

3. Nullifying or sabotaging your intents.

This occurs when you promise and doubt all within the span of a single thought or sentence.

I'm going to make changes at work.... but they will never listen to me anyway,

This also occurs when you use non-committed language that demonstrate you are unsure.

> *I'm going to <u>try</u>*
> *I <u>think</u> I can do this.*
> *I <u>might</u> be able to figure this out.*
> *I'd <u>like</u> for this to work for me.*

Be bold

> *I'm going to do this....*
> *I CAN do this*
> *I am able to figure this out or*
> *I will figure this out. .*
> *I know this will work for me.*
> *This WILL work for me*

When to set Intents

Energetic Cycles of the Planets

You can release and set new intents *anytime* however you can align to the natural cycles of the universe to provide additional energy to your intents or to assist you with the release of that which you don't want. You energy is connected to 'all' so you are always communicating with the universe.

Full Moon : Is a time to release energies. You hold energetic space for 'things' that may no longer serve who you are. The full moon is an excellent time to release this energy to the universe for healing and create space to be filled with new energy of what you **do** want.

New Moon: is a time to set intents for what you want to call into your life. It is a time to acknowledge the gift that you are to this lifetime and speak to the universe in renewed sense of direction and intending what you want the universe to act on.

The anniversary of your birth (Birthday), or the spring equinox is also a powerful time to set intents.

My Beliefs -The universe provides....

I Intend

I have the ability to manifest all that I dream, desire, and decide for I know I Am one with the universe.

The universe provides all that carries me forward with ease, grace and elegance, on my journey and is for my highest divine purpose.

I manifest, I manifest, I manifest.

Core Intention Ideas

Loving partnership

Other relationship intentions (such as children, friends, parents, co-workers, etc.)

Work, career

Physical body, health

Spiritual, etheric

Physical environment, home, business

Mental and emotional being

Play or adventure

Creative or creating

Financial and prosperity

Earth and humanity

Cosmic or global

Writing intents takes thought and practice.

To help you begin, below are examples of both limiting intent and intents that have expansion and allow the universe to provide without limitations.

Career example limiting : I intend to receive a promotion to manager of my department before the end of the year.

Career example open : I intend to create work that is rewarding and exciting, pays more than I can even imagine, has fun and creative co-workers and is ideally located. I intend that this job will make me feel prosperous, joyous, creative, appreciated, respected, excited and eternally thankful !

Money example limiting: I intend to receive a 10% raise this year at review time.

Money example open: I intend to create more than enough money in easy, elegant and fun ways, and for this abundance to fill me with safety, security, freedom and ease. I intend for this money to manifest in perfect timing with harm to none.

Perfect job open examples

I intend to create a job I love that makes me feel excited, creative, prosperous, abundant, joyful and appreciated.

I intend that this job will be filled with fun, positive challenges, and co-workers I love to work with

I intend to be well compensated for this job, with a salary that is more than I had expected. I intend that this job will have ample opportunities for advancement, ongoing education, travel, and schedule flexibility.

I intend that this job I love will be in a place I love, with hours, workdays and a location that fits me perfect.

I intend that this job will be in a beautiful setup with an office that is bright, healthy, clean, vibrant and creative.

Relationship

I intend to create a relationship and life partner that will be as committed to me as I am to them.

I intend to create a deeply loving relationship with a (wo)man.

I intend that this relationship will bring us love, fun, safety, security, laughter, freedom, trust, respect, intimacy and joy.

I intend that my partner shares compatible core and spiritual ideals, values, beliefs and priorities in life's and that he/she has the character and integrity to live by those ideals, priorities and values.

I intend that the (wo)man in my loving partnership is emotionally, physically, and spiritually available.

I intend that the (wo)man in my loving partnership is emotionally mature and of sound mind and body

I intend that the (wo)man in my loving partnership is as committed to creating a caring, loving and growing partnership as I am

I intend that we share compatible ideas of lifestyle, including how to keep and decorate a home, divide chores and spend our free time and how we spend our money

I intend that my loving partner and I are beautifully compatible physically - including our sexual preference, the amount of energy we have, our sleep patterns, our eating habits and the way we spend our physical time together.

I intend to create this loving relationship in a physical area I love that is easy, fun, healthy and joyful for me to reside in.

Health:

I intend that my physical body is 100% vital, healthy and filled with energy.

I intend to keep my body weight at the range of xxx with ease and elegance

I intend to reverse the aging process and fully rejuvenate my physical body.

I intend to look and feel ageless

I intend to be draw to and crave the movement, food/supplements, and body/energetic work that my body needs to stay in perfect shape. I intend that this will have the greatest positive impact on my physical, energetic, spiritual and mental bodies.

Completion

I request and intend to receive help from all of my unseen angels, guides, energetic beings to assist in manifestation of all of my intentions even greater than I have stated, for my highest divine purpose.

In the diagram below define the domains or areas that you'd like to focus. Domain ideas may be home, career, family, relationships, health, or love, and collectively support your existence. These are the areas you want to focus on in setting intents to manifest new energy in these areas. You may use this diagram to focus on one or many areas. You complete this chart, however you may decide to only focus on one domain at this time.

My thoughts are.......

My words create.................

I live ....

My transformation is...................

I begin this great journey to self discovery, and the excitement of what I'm to learn along the way.... I enter this space without fear and with the acknowledgement of the spirit I Am and what I Am able to create.

In the following pages, use the areas you defined for focus (taken from the box diagram on page 53) and write your intents.

Once complete, validate that they align with your I AM declarations that you wrote on page 31.

You are now ready for practice of affirmation of your intents. You are aligned to where you want to focus and your I AM energy.

You will notice that each day has place in the upper right corner where you may log what '**domain focus area**' you are concentrating on. You may focus on one or many, and you may focus on one or many for the duration of this practice.

You may find as you manifest, you will want to, or need to adjust your focus areas or intents.

Where I intend my focus, I AM.

Today I begin my tomorrows with my focus here.. now...

Day 1   _____

My intent for today is:

_____
_____
_____
_____
_____
_____
_____
_____

My actions/feelings at this moment :

_____
_____
_____
_____

My discovery/experience today:

_____
_____
_____
_____
_____
_____
_____
_____
_____

I will not avoid that which is before me as it is to help me learn, grow and transform

Day 2   _____

My intent for today is:

_____

_____

_____

_____

_____

_____

_____

_____

My actions/feelings at this moment :

_____

_____

_____

_____

_____

My discovery/experience today:

_____

_____

_____

_____

_____

_____

_____

_____

_____

I am perfect as I AM

Day 3 _____

My intent for today is:

_____
_____
_____
_____
_____
_____
_____
_____

My actions/feelings at this moment :

_____
_____
_____
_____
_____

My discovery/experience today:

_____
_____
_____
_____
_____
_____
_____
_____
_____

My journey is with intent and purpose..

Day 4   _____

My intent for today is:

_____
_____
_____
_____
_____
_____
_____
_____

My actions/feelings at this moment :

_____
_____
_____
_____
_____

My discovery/experience today:

_____
_____
_____
_____
_____
_____
_____
_____
_____

Become the dance !!!

Day 5 _____

My intent for today is:

_____
_____
_____
_____
_____
_____
_____
_____

My actions/feelings at this moment :

_____
_____
_____
_____
_____

My discovery/experience today:

_____
_____
_____
_____
_____
_____
_____
_____
_____

When I pause, I hear my heart. When I hear my heart I am reminded of this adventure of life..

Day 6 _____

My intent for today is:

_____
_____
_____
_____
_____
_____
_____
_____

My actions/feelings at this moment :

_____
_____
_____
_____

My discovery/experience today:

_____
_____
_____
_____
_____
_____
_____
_____

Wandering has direction unless you walk backward !

Day 7   _____

My intent for today is:

_____
_____
_____
_____
_____
_____
_____
_____

My actions/feelings at this moment :

_____
_____
_____
_____
_____

My discovery/experience today:

_____
_____
_____
_____
_____
_____
_____
_____
_____

Flying !!!

Week 1 - What has manifested for you ?   Are you manifesting what you desire ? Adjust your intents if needed.

Adjustments to focus, intents, or I AM.

Transformation is growth

Day 8 _____

My intent for today is:

_____
_____
_____
_____
_____
_____
_____
_____

My actions/feelings at this moment :

_____
_____
_____
_____
_____

My discovery/experience today:

_____
_____
_____
_____
_____
_____
_____
_____
_____

The universe provides portals for us to enter every day

Day 9 _____

My intent for today is:

_____

_____

_____

_____

_____

_____

_____

_____

My actions/feelings at this moment :

_____

_____

_____

_____

_____

My discovery/experience today:

_____

_____

_____

_____

_____

_____

_____

_____

_____

The universe teaches each day - I learn each day and I am in gratitude for all that is presented

Day 10 _____

My intent for today is:

_____
_____
_____
_____
_____
_____
_____
_____

My actions/feelings at this moment :

_____
_____
_____
_____

My discovery/experience today:

_____
_____
_____
_____
_____
_____
_____
_____
_____

I am perfect, whole and complete

Day 11 _____

My intent for today is:

_____
_____
_____
_____
_____
_____
_____
_____

My actions/feelings at this moment :

_____
_____
_____
_____
_____

My discovery/experience today:

_____
_____
_____
_____
_____
_____
_____
_____
_____

Day 12 _____

My intent for today is:

_____
_____
_____
_____
_____
_____
_____
_____

My actions/feelings at this moment :

_____
_____
_____
_____
_____

My discovery/experience today:

_____
_____
_____
_____
_____
_____
_____
_____
_____

Day 13   _____

My intent for today is:

_____
_____
_____
_____
_____
_____
_____
_____

My actions/feelings at this moment :

_____
_____
_____
_____

My discovery/experience today:

_____
_____
_____
_____
_____
_____
_____
_____

I believe in all that I do, am and aspire to become

Day 14 _____

My intent for today is:

_____
_____
_____
_____
_____
_____
_____
_____

My actions/feelings at this moment :

_____
_____
_____
_____
_____

My discovery/experience today:

_____
_____
_____
_____
_____
_____
_____
_____

Flying Higher !!!

Week 2 - What has manifested for you ? I you are manifesting but it is not exactly what you've asked for - note where you may need clarity in your focus or your intents. Do you intents align with your I AM's ?

Adjustments to focus, intents, or I AM.

*I've chosen freedom in this lifetime, and with that choice
I have the freedom to create my experience*

Day 15 _____

My intent for today is:

_____
_____
_____
_____
_____
_____
_____
_____

My actions/feelings at this moment :

_____
_____
_____
_____
_____

My discovery/experience today:

_____
_____
_____
_____
_____
_____
_____
_____
_____

I am Light, and my light is ignited by all that I do, be and am

Day 16 _____

My intent for today is:

_____
_____
_____
_____
_____
_____
_____
_____

My actions/feelings at this moment :

_____
_____
_____
_____

My discovery/experience today:

_____
_____
_____
_____
_____
_____
_____
_____

I let go !   I let be !

I acknowledge my inner power

Day 17 _____

My intent for today is:

_____

_____

_____

_____

_____

_____

_____

_____

My actions/feelings at this moment :

_____

_____

_____

_____

My discovery/experience today:

_____

_____

_____

_____

_____

_____

_____

_____

My voice speaks my authentic truth

Day 18 _____

My intent for today is:

_____
_____
_____
_____
_____
_____
_____
_____

My actions/feelings at this moment :

_____
_____
_____
_____
_____

My discovery/experience today:

_____
_____
_____
_____
_____
_____
_____
_____
_____

I trust in the universe and all that is provided

Day 19 _____

My intent for today is:

_____
_____
_____
_____
_____
_____
_____
_____

My actions/feelings at this moment :

_____
_____
_____
_____
_____

My discovery/experience today:

_____
_____
_____
_____
_____
_____
_____
_____
_____

I draw to me that which I have asked for

Day 20 _____

My intent for today is:

_____
_____
_____
_____
_____
_____
_____
_____

My actions/feelings at this moment :

_____
_____
_____
_____
_____

My discovery/experience today:

_____
_____
_____
_____
_____
_____
_____
_____

My dreams today are my future reality

Day 21 _____

My intent for today is:

_____
_____
_____
_____
_____
_____
_____
_____

My actions/feelings at this moment :

_____
_____
_____
_____
_____

My discovery/experience today:

_____
_____
_____
_____
_____
_____
_____
_____
_____

Flying with boldness !!!

Week 3 - What has manifested for you ? What new intents might I intend ?

Adjustments to focus, intents, or I AM.

My frequency is elevated to experience all that I desire

Day 22   _____

My intent for today is:

_____
_____
_____
_____
_____
_____
_____
_____

My actions/feelings at this moment :

_____
_____
_____
_____

My discovery/experience today:

_____
_____
_____
_____
_____
_____
_____
_____

I understand and follow my passion freely, openly and with excitement

Day 23 _____

My intent for today is:

_____
_____
_____
_____
_____
_____
_____
_____

My actions/feelings at this moment :

_____
_____
_____
_____

My discovery/experience today:

_____
_____
_____
_____
_____
_____
_____
_____

I Live with Ease, Elegance and Grace

Day 24 _____

My intent for today is:

_____

_____

_____

_____

_____

_____

_____

_____

My actions/feelings at this moment :

_____

_____

_____

_____

_____

My discovery/experience today:

_____

_____

_____

_____

_____

_____

_____

_____

Not making a decision is making a decision....

Day 25   _____

My intent for today is:

_____

_____

_____

_____

_____

_____

_____

_____

My actions/feelings at this moment :

_____

_____

_____

_____

_____

My discovery/experience today:

_____

_____

_____

_____

_____

_____

_____

_____

All is as it is meant to be

Day 26 _____

My intent for today is:

_____
_____
_____
_____
_____
_____
_____
_____

My actions/feelings at this moment :

_____
_____
_____
_____
_____

My discovery/experience today:

_____
_____
_____
_____
_____
_____
_____
_____
_____

I'm living my dream !!

Day 27   _____

My intent for today is:

_____
_____
_____
_____
_____
_____
_____
_____

My actions/feelings at this moment :

_____
_____
_____
_____

My discovery/experience today:

_____
_____
_____
_____
_____
_____
_____
_____

I dream, I dream, I dream ......

Day 28 _____

My intent for today is:

_____
_____
_____
_____
_____
_____
_____
_____

My actions/feelings at this moment :

_____
_____
_____
_____
_____

My discovery/experience today:

_____
_____
_____
_____
_____
_____
_____
_____
_____

Soaring !!!

Week 4 - Completion !

Adjustments to focus, intents, or I AM ?

What has manifested for you ? Am I complete ?

Create Your Personal Daily Intent :

Daily Intent -

By the powers of the East - which have ably mastered all adversity
By the Powers of the West - where there are no obstacles to my will
By the Powers of the North -where luck smiles upon me every day of the year
By the Powers of the South - where all my desires are immediately granted

I seek that my life be free from all negative thoughts and actions. My close family, my friends, my employers my employees are happy
My projects, my hopes, my dreams, my business, my work is excellent and fun
My meals, my food is delicious and healthy

I don't wish to be younger, nor to be older
I want to benefit ardently from the present hour and the present day. I am full of kindness for the whole world and I expect nothing in exchange for the love that I give

I wish that the abundance, strength, confidence and attractions born of my thoughts, my words, my actions flood all of my life and, that everything I touch changes into treasure   So note it be.

Laurie Wondra - YourLifeCore

Closure and Blessing

Set your life intents for living in a new energy field, embracing all that the universe provides to you. Renew and modify those intents as you continue on your journey within this lifetime. May you learn that working with your energy gives you a new way of being within the universal energy of higher consciousness.

Love and light to you as you journey.

And so it is,
so be it,
and so I Am, I Am, I Am.

Notes :

_____

_____

_____

_____

_____

_____

_____

_____

_____

_____

_____

_____

_____

_____

_____

_____

_____

_____

_____

_____

_____

_____

_____

_____

_____

_____

_____

Notes :

Notes :

Notes :

_____
_____
_____
_____
_____
_____
_____
_____
_____
_____
_____
_____
_____
_____
_____
_____
_____
_____
_____
_____
_____
_____
_____

Notes :

Notes :

Closure

We are magnificent energetic beings. Our souls have agreed to be here to traverse the experiences of the universe. We are brave and courageous as we continue on this journey of transformation of our energy. We are to experience the realization of our magnificence as human beings as we mingle and adjust with the environment elements and souls around us.

It is this wondrous dance we do and we are here to enjoy this dance, to explore, experiences and celebrate in infinite joy, peace, love, abundance and the ability to manifest our creative desires.

Continued Practices

I AM !

I AM Perfection

I AM Transforming

I AM Loved

I AM

I AM

I AM

I AM

I AM

I AM

I AM

I AM

I AM

I AM

I AM

I AM

I AM

I AM

Extra : In the diagram below define the domains or areas that you'd like to focus. Domain ideas may be home, career, family, relationships, health, or love, and collectively support your existence. These are the areas you want to focus on in setting intents to manifest new energy in these areas. You may use this diagram to focus on one or many areas. You complete this chart, however you may decide to only focus on one domain at this time.

I Intend :

In loving peace. joy. love and manifestation.............

In loving peace, joy, love and manifestation.............

In loving peace, joy, love and manifestation.............

Made in the USA
Charleston, SC
20 December 2016